Flavours of WILTSHIRE

RECIPES

Compiled by Julia Skinner

THE FRANCIS FRITH COLLECTION

www.francisfrith.com

First published in the United Kingdom in 2012 by The Francis Frith Collection®

This edition published exclusively for Bradwell Books in 2012
For trade enquiries see: www.bradwellbooks.com or tel: 0800 834 920
ISBN 978-1-84589-691-1

Text and Design copyright The Francis Frith Collection®
Photographs copyright The Francis Frith Collection® except where indicated.

The Frith® photographs and the Frith® logo are reproduced under licence from
Heritage Photographic Resources Ltd, the owners of the Frith® archive and trademarks.
'The Francis Frith Collection', 'Francis Frith' and 'Frith' are registered trademarks of
Heritage Photographic Resources Ltd.

British Library Cataloguing in Publication Data

Flavours of Wiltshire - Recipes
Compiled by Julia Skinner

The Francis Frith Collection
Oakley Business Park,
Wylye Road, Dinton,
Wiltshire SP3 5EU
Tel: +44 (0) 1722 716 376
Email: info@francisfrith.co.uk

www.francisfrith.com

Printed and bound in Malaysia
Contains material sourced from responsibly managed forests

Front Cover: **CORSHAM, MEN OUTSIDE THE ALMSHOUSES 1906** 54353p
Frontispiece: **BLUNSDON, LOWER VILLAGE ROAD 1911** B293003
Contents: **BRADFORD-ON-AVON, CHURCH STREET c1945** B174012

The colour-tinting is for illustrative purposes only, and is not intended to be historically accurate

CONTENTS

RECIPE

MARLBOROUGH SHEEP FAIR DAY SOUP

Huge flocks of sheep grazed on Salisbury Plain and the downs of north Wiltshire in the past, reared for both meat and wool. One of the most important events in the year for Wiltshire shepherds was the large sheep fair held in August at Tan Hill on the Marlborough Downs above the village of All Cannings, where thousands of sheep were brought from a wide area to be bought and sold. The recipe for this soup was recorded in J A Leete's 'Wiltshire Miscellany' (1975) as a tasty and economical dish that was made by the sheep-keeping communities on the Marlborough Downs and traditionally eaten by the shepherd and his family after arriving home from the Marlborough Sheep Fair. Although it is called a soup it is actually more like a thin stew, and was often served as such with boiled potatoes. This amount should make 6-8 bowlfuls.

> 225g/8oz lean mutton or lamb (from the neck, shoulder or leg)
> 2 large or 3 medium onions, peeled and thinly sliced
> 225g/8oz peas, fresh or frozen
> 1 mugful finely shredded lettuce (such as Little Gem or Cos),
>   or shredded green cabbage or spring or winter greens can
>   be used if preferred
> 600ml/1 pint water
> Salt and pepper

Trim the meat of any excess fat and cut it into very small pieces. Put the meat in a large saucepan with the peas, sliced onions and lettuce or cabbage. Add the water and season well with plenty of salt and pepper. Bring to the boil, then reduce the heat, cover the pan and leave it to cook gently at a low heat for at least one hour, but a longer cooking time will only improve the flavour. Serve this either as a soup, accompanied with crusty bread, or as a stew, served with boiled potatoes.

BURBAGE, THE VILLAGE 1907 57208

RECIPE

WATERCRESS SOUP

Traditionally-grown watercress is cultivated in flowing watercourses of mineral-rich water of the highest purity, and the clear chalk streams of Wiltshire are ideal for growing it. Watercress has been eaten in Britain for centuries, but in earlier times it was mainly valued for its medicinal properties. It was only adopted into the general diet in the early 19th century, when it began to be commercially and hygienically produced in large quantities; it became very popular, and huge amounts of watercress were sent by train to the markets of London, Birmingham and Manchester. Watercress beds were once prolific in Wiltshire and watercress is still produced by a few commercial growers in the county, such as John Hurd's Organic Watercress at Hill Deverill, south of Warminster, and Chalke Valley Watercress at Broadchalke, west of Salisbury. Watercress is a super-food packed with nutrients, with a distinctive peppery, slightly bitter, flavour. It can be eaten raw as a salad or in sandwiches or used to make a sauce to accompany freshwater fish, but is best known for making a delicious soup.

50g/2oz butter
2 bags or bunches of watercress with their stalks removed, washed
   and finely chopped (but reserve a few sprigs to garnish the soup)
1 medium onion, chopped
25g/1oz plain flour
600ml/1 pint milk
450ml/¾ pint chicken or vegetable stock
Salt and pepper
6 tablespoonfuls single cream

Melt the butter in a large pan, and gently fry the watercress and onion for a few minutes until softened. Stir in the flour and cook for a further one minute. Slowly stir in the milk, a little at a time, and then the stock. Bring to the boil, stirring all the time, until thickened, season to taste, then cover and simmer gently for 30 minutes. Remove from the heat and cool for a few minutes, then liquidize. Before serving, add the cream and reheat gently, taking care not to allow the soup to boil. Check the seasoning and serve with a swirl of cream and a sprig of watercress leaves to garnish.

SALISBURY
THE CATHEDRAL
1906 56363

Wiltshire's chalk streams and rivers also provide the clear, fast-running water required by brown trout. The Kennet has been famous for its trout since the 17th century, and the Victoria County History of Wiltshire (volume 4) records the local legend that in the 16th century Queen Elizabeth I regularly breakfasted on trout from the River Ebble in the south of the county whilst staying at Wilton House, west of Salisbury. Nowadays there are also a number of fish farms in the county where both native brown trout and rainbow trout are reared, such as Trafalgar Fisheries at Downton, near Salisbury, which supplies the retail and food sector market, and Mere Fish Farm at Ivymead near Mere, in the extreme south-west corner of the county near the borders of Somerset and Dorset, and close to the beautiful National Trust property of Stourhead. Mere Fish Farm's products are sold at a number of local outlets and farmers' markets in Wiltshire, Somerset and Dorset – check their website for details: www.merefishfarm.co.uk. Both these businesses not only supply fresh trout but also produce smoked trout, which is used in the recipe on the opposite page to make a smoked trout paté.

STOURHEAD, THE PLEASURE GARDENS c1965 S741096

RECIPE

SMOKED TROUT PATÉ

If smoked trout proves hard to find, this can also be made with smoked mackerel fillets instead. If necessary this can be prepared a day in advance and kept in the refrigerator until required. Serves 4-6.

> 225g/8oz soft cream cheese, such as Philadelphia
>   or equivalent
> 225g/8oz smoked trout fillets
> Finely grated rind of half a lemon
> 1 tablespoonful lemon juice
> 2 teaspoonfuls horseradish sauce
> A good pinch of Cayenne pepper
> Freshly ground black pepper
> 1 tablespoonful finely chopped fresh parsley

Flake the trout, discarding the skin and any bones. Put the soft cheese and lemon rind into a blender or food processor. Add the flaked fish and blend until smooth. Add the horseradish sauce, Cayenne pepper, black pepper and lemon juice and blend briefly. Spoon into either 4-6 individual ramekin dishes or one serving dish, cover with cling film and chill in the refrigerator for at least one hour before serving.

Garnish each portion with a sprinkling of freshly chopped parsley before serving with crusty bread, toast or crackers.

RECIPE

Brinkworth Blue Cheese and Broccoli Flan

The saying 'as different as chalk and cheese' originated in Wiltshire in the contrast between the landscape, geology and agriculture of the county in past times. The chalkland of the south was sheep and corn country, whereas dairy farming was the mainstay of the flat, rich pastures to the north and west. The dairies of this region were renowned for their North Wiltshire Cheese, a hard-pressed, close-textured cheese similar to Gloucester. Large cheeses were known as North Wiltshire and smaller ones were called Wiltshire Loaves. North Wiltshire Cheese was very popular in the past – it has been estimated that in 1798 over 5,000 tons was made – but the county's cheese-making tradition died out in the early 20th century and North Wiltshire cheese became extinct. However, in recent years the making of North Wiltshire cheese has been revived by Ceri and Chad Cryer of the Brinkworth Dairy at Hill End Farm, Brinkworth, in the Dauntsey Vale between Malmesbury and Wootton Bassett. They sell their North Wiltshire Loaf and other cheeses they produce at local shops and farmers' markets as well as online via their website – www.ceris-cheese.co.uk. They also make a nice blue cheese called Brinkworth Blue, which is used here to make a savoury flan that can be eaten warm or cold. If you can't get Brinkworth Blue, this recipe also works well with Stilton or Shropshire Blue cheese.

175g/6oz plain flour
75g/3oz butter or margarine
225g/8oz trimmed weight of broccoli florets
175g/6oz Brinkworth Blue cheese, or alternative,
   cut into small pieces
3 eggs, beaten
300ml/½ pint single cream
Salt and freshly ground black pepper

Grease a flan tin about 23-26cms (9-10 ins) in diameter. Put the flour in a mixing bowl with a pinch of salt and rub in the butter or margarine. Mix in 2-3 tablespoonfuls of cold water, just enough to form a firm dough, then knead the dough lightly until it is smooth and elastic. Roll it out on a lightly floured surface and line the flan tin, then put it in the fridge to chill for 15 minutes. Pre-heat the oven to 190°C/375°F/Gas Mark 5.

Prick the pastry base all over with a fork to allow air bubbles to escape during cooking. Line the pastry case with a piece of greaseproof paper and fill with baking beans or dry rice. Bake blind in the oven for 10-15 minutes, until the pastry is just firm and lightly golden. Remove from the oven, take out the beans or rice and paper and return to the oven for 5-7 minutes to dry out the base. Remove from the oven, reduce the oven temperature to 180°C/350°F/Gas Mark 4, and place a baking tray in the oven to heat up.

Bring a pan of water to a fast boil, and add the trimmed broccoli florets. Bring the water back to the boil, cook for 2 minutes, then remove from the heat and drain the broccoli thoroughly. Arrange the broccoli florets in the pastry case, and scatter the pieces of cheese over and around them. Lightly beat together the eggs and cream, and season to taste with salt and plenty of pepper (go easy on the salt if you are using Stilton as an alternative cheese, as this will already be quite salty). Pour the mixture over the broccoli and cheese in the pastry case. Place on the baking tray in the oven (this helps the pastry base to cook through) and bake at the reduced temperature for 30-40 minutes, until the flan is cooked but not dry and the filling is risen and just firm to the touch. Leave the flan to cool a little and eat it warm, or otherwise leave to cool down completely before eating. Either way, it is best eaten the same day as it is cooked.

CHISELDON, HODSON ROAD c1914   C220502

A round North Wiltshire cheese is part of the origin for the nickname of 'Moonrakers' which was given to Wiltshire folk in the past. The story goes that on the night of a full moon, some men from Bishops Cannings in the Vale of Pewsey were busily transporting smuggled kegs of brandy hidden in a wagon-load of hay when they heard the sound of approaching excise men. As quickly as they could, they extracted the kegs and threw them into a nearby pond. The excise men were put off, but not fooled – they left, but doubled back to discover the smugglers attempting to recover the submerged kegs with hay rakes. When asked what they were doing, the smugglers indicated the clear reflection of the full moon shining in the water like a great golden cheese and uttered something like 'Zomebody 'ave lost thic thur cheese and we'm a-rakin for un in thic thur pond'. The excise men smiled at the country simpletons and went on their way, leaving the moonrakers free to go home – and enjoy their brandy.

RECIPE

CHEESE PUDDING

Cheese Pudding used to be a popular dish all over the country. This is a version from Wiltshire. It is a rich and tasty dish which is good eaten either hot or cold, perhaps served with brown bread and butter, or with a salad. The secret to a good Cheese Pudding is to use a tasty, well-flavoured cheese of choice, such as Cheddar, Cheshire, Double Gloucester, Lancashire or even North Wiltshire Loaf, if you can get it. Serves 4.

> 115g/4oz well-flavoured hard cheese of choice, grated
> 50g/2oz fresh bread crumbs
> 300ml/½ pint milk
> 2 eggs, beaten
> Salt and pepper
> ½ teaspoonful made mustard

Put the grated cheese and breadcrumbs into a basin. Heat the milk and pour it over the cheese and breadcrumbs. Mix it all well together then leave to stand for one hour, for the breadcrumbs to soak up the liquid.

Pre-heat the oven to 180°C/350°F/Gas Mark 4. Grease a shallow ovenproof dish of about 900ml/1½ pints capacity. Stir the beaten eggs into the mixture and season to taste with pepper and just a little salt if necessary, as the cheese will already make the dish salty. Stir in the mustard. Pour the mixture into the prepared dish and bake in the pre-heated oven for about 25-30 minutes, until the pudding is well risen and firm to the touch, and the top is starting to brown.

RECIPE

POTATO PIE

This makes a vegetable accompaniment to serve with a main course.
Serves 4-6.

> 900g/2 lbs potatoes, peeled and thinly sliced
> 25g/1oz plain flour
> Salt and pepper
> 600-900ml/1-1½ pints milk
> 25g/1oz butter

Pre-heat the oven to 190°C/375°F/ Gas Mark 5. Put the sliced potatoes
in a bowl, sprinkle with flour and toss so that all sides are coated with
flour. Use a little of the butter to grease a large, shallow ovenproof
dish. Arrange the slices in layers in the dish, seasoning each layer
well with salt and pepper, then pour in enough milk to cover. Dot the
top with small pieces of butter. Cover the dish with a piece of lightly
buttered kitchen foil. Bake in the oven for 1- 1½ hours, until the
potatoes are really tender. Remove the foil and return to the oven for
a further 20-30 minutes, until the top is golden brown.

**RAMSBURY, BURDETT STREET
1906** 57200

RECIPE

WILTSHIRE TATTIES

This is an old Wiltshire way of cooking large 'tatties', or potatoes, which makes a tasty snack or supper dish. If you find the flavouring of lemon and nutmeg in the potato filling too strong, try making this with about 115g/4oz grated Cheddar cheese instead. Serves 4.

> 4 large floury baking potatoes of even size,
>   such as King Edward or Maris Piper
> A little oil or butter
> A little salt (optional)
> 4 level tablespoonfuls fresh brown breadcrumbs
> 115g/4oz Wiltshire ham, finely chopped
> 75g/3oz butter, softened to room temperature
> 1 teaspoonful finely grated lemon rind
> 1 tablespoonful finely chopped fresh parsley
> ¼ teaspoonful ground nutmeg
> Salt and freshly ground black pepper

Pre-heat the oven to 200°C/400°F/Gas Mark 6.

Scrub and dry the potatoes, and prick the skins with a fork to prevent them bursting during cooking. Rub the skins with a little oil or butter and sprinkle over a little salt, if using. Put the potatoes in the hot oven, either on a baking sheet or straight on the oven shelf. Cook for 1-1½ hours until they are soft throughout – test by inserting a sharp knife into the centre.

Allow the potatoes to cool for a while, then cut a piece off the end of each one and carefully scoop out all the potato into a bowl. Mash the potato roughly with a fork, then mix in all the other ingredients and combine well. Fill the hollowed out potato skins with the mixture, then flatten the end of each potato slightly to make a base so that they will stand upright. Stand the filled potatoes in the greased baking tin or ovenproof dish, return to the oven and bake at 200°C/400°F/Gas Mark 6 for 20 minutes.

Wiltshire has been famous for pig farming for centuries and pig products feature highly in the traditional food of the county. Swindon is recorded in the Domesday Book of 1086 as 'Suindune', which is believed to derive from the Anglo-Saxon words for 'swine hill', meaning the place where pigs were kept. Swindon is now a unitary authority but is still the largest town in the ceremonial county of Wiltshire, but in the early 19th century it was just a quiet market town with a population of about 1,200. Then, in the 1830s, the tracks of the Great Western Railway were laid through the fields two miles to the north of the town, and it was here that the railway engineers Isambard Kingdom Brunel and Daniel Gooch decided to establish the GWR locomotion workshops, along with housing for the workers, making Swindon a centre for heavy industry and engineering and triggering its growth into the busy modern town it is today. There is a local legend that when Brunel and Gooch were surveying the area north of Swindon Hill, Brunel threw a sandwich and declared that the spot where it landed would be the location of the works.

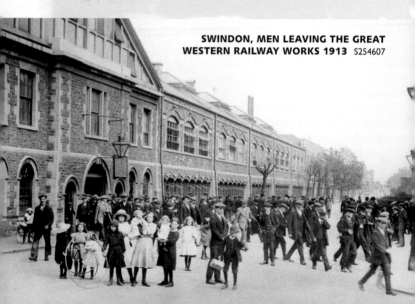

SWINDON, MEN LEAVING THE GREAT WESTERN RAILWAY WORKS 1913 S254607

BY APPOINTMENT
BACON CURERS TO
HIS LATE MAJESTY
KING GEORGE VI
C & T HARRIS (Calne) Ltd.

HARRIS BACON

EST. 1770 at CALNE, WILTS, ENG.

Wiltshire has long been a centre of the ham and bacon industry, and the county is particularly famous for the 'Wiltshire cure', which produces sweet-flavoured mild bacon, smoked or unsmoked. The special cuts and ways of curing which distinguish Wiltshire ham and bacon have been particularly associated with two companies in the county, C & T Harris in Calne and Bowyers in Trowbridge. The Harris family bacon business in Calne was the most important industry in the town for nearly 150 years until it closed in 1982. Calne was blessed with good canal and rail links which helped the Harris business expand, and Wiltshire Cure bacon and hams became famous throughout the country.

What started as a small family concern in 1808, run by Abraham Bowyer, became over the next 200 years one of the largest businesses in Trowbridge. Bowyer started by selling his cured bacon and sausages from the front of his baker's and grocer's shop in Fore Street. The killing and curing took place in the back. Abraham's son Elijah joined the business and it continued to expand. After Abraham's death in 1873 the name Bowyer & Son was retained, and the company continued trading as 'Cheese & Corn Factors, Mealmen and Provision Dealers'. By 1880 Elijah was concentrating on the bacon curing side. In the 1880s he took on J R Philpott and J Sawyer as partners, and a limited company was formed in 1891. The Bowyers factory expanded until it eventually occupied a site covering about 7 acres at the Innox in the centre of Trowbridge. In 1970, when it became Bowyers (Wiltshire) Ltd, the company was one of the biggest producers of sausages and pies in the country. The company then underwent several mergers and acquisitions to become part of Pork Farms Bowyers, but the Trowbridge factory was closed in 2008 and the company's products are now made elsewhere in the country.

RECIPE

BEANS AND BACON

I tell ee what it is me bwoys,
You mid praise beef, and mutton,
An geam, an pawltry, an zish like
Ta I, teant woth a button.

Now var a veed jist let I have,
An dwoant ee be mistaken,
Tha vinest veast in ael the wordle,
Is one, a beeans an beakin.

When you'm at work apon the varm
A mawin, ar haymeakin,
Ther's nuthen that ull stan be ee,
Like a veed a beeans an beakin.

(From 'Wiltshire Rhymes' by Edward Slow, published in 1894).

Beans and Bacon was a staple dish of poorer families all over Britain in the past, and was the original version of the ubiquitous canned baked beans of modern times. It is a filling and inexpensive meal and can be made with either bacon or streaky belly pork. It is easy to make – you just need to remember to soak the beans overnight before use, and then give this dish a long, slow cooking time. Soaking and cooking dried beans gives the best results, but if you don't want to bother with that you can use 2 x 400g cans of haricot beans instead, drained to give about 450g/1 lb weight of beans. This amount will serve 3-4 people, so increase the quantities for more people.

225g/8oz dried haricot beans
25g/1oz butter
175g/6oz bacon lardons, or de-rinded bacon rashers
  or streaky belly pork, cut into pieces
1 onion, peeled but left whole
1 heaped tablespoonful soft brown sugar
½ teaspoonful salt
1 teaspoonful dry mustard powder
2 tablespoonfuls tomato purée

Soak the beans in plenty of cold water overnight before using.
When ready to make this dish, drain the beans and put them in a
large saucepan with enough cold water to cover them by 3cms (1
inch). Bring slowly to the boil, then reduce the heat and simmer
for 1-1½ hours until the beans are almost tender. Drain the beans,
but reserve the liquid as this will be used later. Melt half the
butter in a frying pan and add the bacon or pork pieces. Fry them
for 3-4 minutes, turning them over once or twice. Tip the bacon or
pork and all the fat in the pan into a deep casserole or ovenproof
dish. Pour in the beans and push the peeled, whole onion into the
middle. In a bowl, mix together the sugar, remaining butter, salt,
mustard powder and tomato purée. Gradually stir in the bean
liquid and mix it all to a runny paste, then pour it over the beans.
Cover the dish with its lid and cook in the oven at 150°C/300°F/
Gas Mark 2 for 2½-3 hours, the longer you can cook this the
better it will be. Check after 2 hours, and add a little more water if
it is looking too dry. Remove the lid and cook uncovered for the
last 20 minutes of cooking time.

RECIPE

BACON FRAIZE

Also known as Bacon Froize, this is a very old English dish that dates back to medieval times. A fraize is a batter-like mixture, which was probably originally cooked in the hot fat that dripped from a spit-roasted joint. This is a tasty and economical recipe that stretches one egg and a small amount of bacon between several people. It makes a good breakfast dish, especially if it is served with mushrooms and grilled tomatoes. Serves 2-4, depending on appetite.

> 4 rashers streaky bacon, de-rinded and cut into small pieces
> 50g/2oz plain flour
> 1 egg
> 150ml/¼ pint fresh milk
> Salt and freshly ground black pepper

Pre-heat the oven to 220°C/425°F/Gas Mark 7. Grease an ovenproof dish or dish or tin about 20cms (8ins) square or equivalent and place it in the oven to heat up.

Gently cook the bacon in a non-stick frying pan until the fat runs and the bacon is crisp. Take the dish or tin out of the oven, tip in the bacon and any fat in the pan and spread it evenly over the bottom.

Sift the flour into a bowl. Break in the egg and stir it into the flour, then gradually stir in the milk, beating the mixture well to form a smooth batter. Season to taste with salt and pepper. Pour the batter over the bacon pieces. Bake in the oven for 25-30 minutes until the batter is well risen and golden. Cut into squares or wedges and serve, perhaps with a little mustard.

**LACOCK, WOMEN
IN THE MEDIEVAL
PAGEANT 1932**
L1505

19

GENTLEMEN

Pears

PASSENGERS ARE REQUESTED
TO CROSS THE LINE
BY THE BRIDGE ONLY

RECIPE

Beef Braised in Wiltshire Beer

'...so he had his little table drawn out close to the fire, and fell to work upon a well cooked steak and smoking hot potatoes, with a strong appreciation of their excellence, and a very keen sense of enjoyment. Beside him, too, stood a jug of most stupendous Wiltshire beer.'
(From 'Martin Chuzzlewit' by Charles Dickens, 1844)

As seen in the above quote, the good malting barley grown in Wiltshire made the county renowned for its beer in the 19th century, and its brewing tradition still continues – a famous Wiltshire brewery name is Wadworth of Devizes, brewers of such popular cask ales as 6X, Henry's Original IPA and The Bishop's Tipple, but there are also a number of smaller breweries around the county that produce an excellent brew. Use your own favourite Wiltshire beer to make this tasty beef stew to serve with boiled, mashed or baked potatoes and seasonal vegetables.

900g/2 lbs lean braising or stewing steak, cut into cubes
425ml/15 fl oz/¾ pint beer or ale of choice
1 tablespoonful cooking oil
3 medium sized onions, peeled and cut into quarters
2 garlic cloves, peeled and crushed or very finely chopped
1 rounded tablespoonful plain flour
1 teaspoonful dried mixed herbs
2 bay leaves
Salt and freshly ground black pepper

Pre-heat the oven to 150°C/300°F/Gas Mark 2. Heat the oil in a large frying pan and fry the cubes of meat in small batches, a few pieces at a time, until they are well browned on all sides. As you brown the meat, remove it to a plate. When all the meat has been browned, put the sliced onions in the pan and fry until they are lightly browned at the edges, stirring them around as they cook. Add the garlic and let that cook for a minute or so, then reduce the heat and return the meat to the pan and sprinkle over the flour. Stir around with a wooden spoon until all the flour has been absorbed into the pan juices. Gradually stir in the beer, a little at a time, then turn up the heat and bring it all to simmering point, stirring continually, until the sauce has thickened and starting to bubble. Add the mixed herbs, bay leaves and salt and pepper to taste. Pour it into a large casserole dish, cover with its lid and cook in the centre of the pre-heated oven for a full 2½ hours to allow the beer to mellow and develop into a flavoursome sauce.

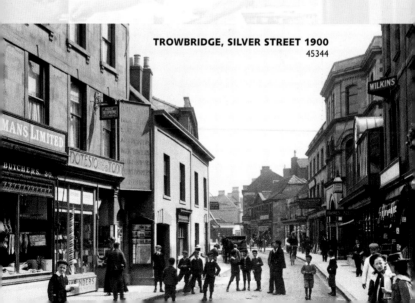

TROWBRIDGE, SILVER STREET 1900
45344

WOOTTON BASSETT, THE MARKET, HIGH STREET 1906 WI71507

Wiltshire's country towns were busy places on market day in the past, as can be seen in the view of Wootton Bassett in 1906 above. Farmers from all around the area thronged to their local market town to buy and sell their livestock and then treated themselves to dinner at a local inn or tavern before going home.

RECIPE

MARKET DAY DINNER

This is the sort of hearty meal, known as a 'farmer's ordinary', that would be served to farmers on market day in local inns. Long, slow cooking is the secret to making this tasty hot-pot style dish. Serves 4.

> 4 pork chops, with their bones and fat trimmed off
> 2 pigs' kidneys, cored and sliced
> 2 onions, peeled and thinly sliced
> 1 large cooking apple, peeled, cored and sliced
> 1 teaspoonful chopped sage, fresh or dried
> Salt and pepper
> 675g/1½ lbs potatoes, peeled and thinly sliced
> 450ml/¾ pint chicken or vegetable stock
>   (or half stock and half cider, if preferred)
> 25g/1oz butter, melted

Pre-heat the oven to 160°C/325°F/Gas Mark 3. Put half the sliced potatoes and onions in the bottom of a very large ovenproof casserole. Cover with the pork chops and sliced kidneys, and then the sliced apple and the rest of the onions. Sprinkle over the sage, and season well with salt and pepper. Cover it all with an overlapping layer of the remaining sliced potatoes. Pour over the stock, or stock and cider. Cover the dish with its lid and cook in the pre-heated oven for 2-2½ hours, until the potatoes are tender and cooked through and most of the stock has been absorbed. Remove the lid and brush the potato topping with melted butter. Return to the oven and cook, uncovered, for a further 30 minutes for the potatoes to crisp and brown at the edges.

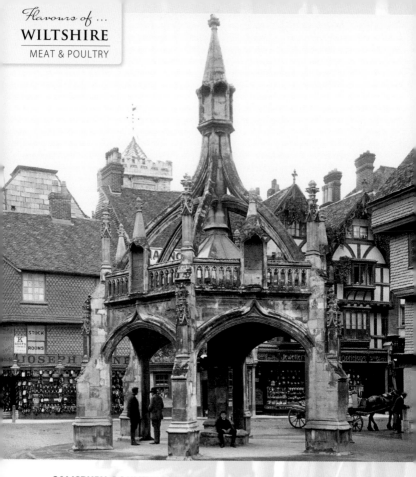

SALISBURY, POULTRY CROSS AND SILVER STREET 1906 56359

This shows the beautiful hexagonal Poultry Cross that stands in the centre of Salisbury, which dates from the 15th century. There were originally four medieval market crosses in the city, but Poultry Cross, at the junction of Butcher Row and Minster Street, is the only one to have survived. It marked the area that was reserved for the selling of poultry and vegetables.

26

RECIPE

CHICKEN AND HAM LOAF

450g/1 lb raw chicken breast
450g/1 lb cooked ham
115g/4oz fresh white breadcrumbs
2 eggs, beaten
150ml/¼ pint double cream
2 tablespoonfuls finely chopped fresh parsley
A pinch of grated nutmeg
Salt and pepper
6-8 rashers streaky bacon, rind removed

Pre-heat the oven to 190°C/375°C/Gas Mark 5 and grease a 900g/2lb loaf tin.

Mince the chicken and ham, or chop it into very small pieces. Add the breadcrumbs and mix again. Add in the beaten eggs, cream, parsley, nutmeg and seasonings and combine it all together well. Lightly stretch the bacon rashers then use them to line the greased loaf tin, overlapping them slightly, and let any extra length hang over the edge. Fill the tin with the mixture, press it down lightly to firm it and smooth the top. Bring any protruding lengths of bacon rashers over the top of the filling. Cover the top of the tin securely with a piece of buttered kitchen foil and stand the tin in a roasting tin filled with enough very hot water to come halfway up its sides. Bake in the pre-heated oven for 1¼ hours, topping up the tin with more hot water if necessary, then remove the foil lid and bake for a further 15 minutes. Remove from the oven and leave in the tin for 30 minutes, then turn out onto a plate. This can be eaten hot or cold, served cut into thick slices.

GIPSYUN AT STOUNHENGE

Zo wen tha day wur drawin ni,
There wur zich fussen mang the maids,
A meakin zich gurt pies an cakes,
Ta want we wur nar bit afraid.

A gir big piece of beef they'd cook'd,
An sich a woppin ham had bought,
They wur obliged ta cut un droo,
To get un in the biggest pot.

STONEHENGE, FROM THE EAST 1887 19796

Zo Fan did spread a girt big cloth
Apon tha grass, an we zat down,
An mead shart wirk of beef an ham,
Vor appetites we ael ad voun.

An we did ate and drink za long,
Till nothin skierce wur left bit bounes,
Then we got up ta look about,
An zee tha girt big hanshint stones.

(From 'Wiltshire Rhymes', Edward Stow, published in 1894)

RECIPE

WILTSHIRE PLAIT

This is rather like a giant sausage roll and is good eaten either hot or cold. Use belly pork which has an equal amount of lean meat and fat, and a mature, well-flavoured Cheddar cheese. Serves 4.

275g/10oz belly pork, minced, or chopped into very small pieces
50g/2oz cooking apple, peeled, cored and chopped into small pieces
50g/2oz mature cheddar cheese, grated
50g/2oz onion, peeled and finely chopped
1 garlic clove, peeled and crushed or very finely chopped
5 tablespoonfuls finely chopped fresh broadleaf parsley
Salt and freshly ground black pepper
1 egg, beaten
350g/12oz prepared puff pastry

Pre-heat the oven to 220°C/425°F/Gas Mark 7 and grease a baking sheet.

Mix together the pork, apple, cheese, onion, garlic, parsley and half the beaten egg, and season well with salt and finely ground black pepper.

Roll out the pastry to about 23-26cms (9-10 ins) square. Flour your hands and form the meat mixture into a loaf shape about 8 x 20cms (3 x 8ins) and lay it in the centre of the pastry square. Cut the pastry on either side of it into diagonal strips 1cm (½ inch) wide. Dampen the end of each strip, then fold the strips alternately over the meat loaf from side to side to create a plaited, lattice effect in a criss-cross pattern over the filling, sealing the ends down firmly to the pastry on the other side. Brush all over the pastry with the remaining beaten egg. Carefully slide the Plait onto a dampened baking sheet (this helps the pastry to puff) and bake in the pre-heated oven for 20 minutes, then reduce the oven temperature to 180°C/350°F/Gas Mark 4 and bake for a further 20-25 minutes.

RECIPE

WILTSHIRE PUDDING

This is based on a recipe for Wiltshire Pudding that was included by a Mrs Dalgairns in her book 'The Practice of Cookery: Adapted to the Business of Every Day Life', 3rd edition, Edinburgh and London, 1830. Her recipe was originally for a steamed pudding, but this has been adapted to bake in the oven, with the addition of a little sugar which Mrs Dalgairns did not include, and makes a delicious sponge pudding with a crispy top. The mixture of redcurrants and raspberries that Mrs Dalgairns used in her original pudding is a lovely flavoursome combination of soft summer fruits, but later in the year you could go foraging in the Wiltshire countryside for blackberries to use instead, to make a seasonal autumn pudding.

> 175g/6oz self-raising flour
> 75g/3oz butter, softened to room temperature
> 50g/2oz caster sugar
> 1 egg, beaten
> 115g/4oz redcurrants, stripped off their stalks
> 115g/4oz raspberries
> About 150ml/5fl oz/¼ pint milk

Pre-heat the oven to 180°C/350°F/Gas Mark 4 and grease an ovenproof dish of at least 1.2 litre/2 pint capacity.

Sift the flour into a mixing bowl. Rub in the butter until the mixture resembles fine breadcrumbs, then stir in the sugar. Make a well in the centre and add the egg and enough of the milk to mix it all together well into a smooth mixture with a soft dropping consistency. Gently stir in the soft fruit, then pour the mixture into the prepared dish. Bake, uncovered, in the pre-heated oven for one hour, until well risen and firm to the touch – don't take it out too early or the base of the pudding might not be cooked through properly. Check the pudding after 45 minutes and cover the top with a piece of kitchen foil if it seems to be browning too quickly, then continue cooking for the rest of the time.

RECIPE

MARLBOROUGH PUDDING-PIE

This recipe is named after Marlborough, a charming Wiltshire town which boasts one of the widest high streets in the country, eminently suited to busy market days in the past. Some recipes for Marlborough Pudding-Pie have a layer of mixed candied peel beneath the baked custard-style topping, but this version using jam is the one that the Victorian cookery guru Mrs Beeton featured in her famous 'Book of Household Management' of 1861.

> 175g/6oz prepared puff pastry.
> 115g/4oz butter, softened
> 115g/4oz caster sugar
> 4 eggs, beaten
> Enough jam to spread over the base of the pie – any flavour of choice, but apricot jam works particularly well in this pudding, and does not discolour the set custard topping.

Pre-heat the oven to 180°C/350°F/Gas Mark 4 and place a baking tray in the oven to heat up. Grease a pie dish about 20-22cms (8-9ins) in diameter.

Roll out the pastry and use it to line the greased pie dish. Spread a layer of jam across the base.

Beat together the softened butter and sugar until the mixture is light and fluffy. Gradually mix in the beaten eggs, a little at a time to prevent the mixture curdling, and beating well after each addition, then pour the mixture into the pie dish. Place the pie dish on the baking tray in the pre-heated oven (this helps the pastry base to cook through) and bake for 35-40 minutes, until the filling is golden brown, well-risen and firm. Remove from the oven and leave to settle for a few minutes before serving.

MARLBOROUGH, TOWN HALL 1902 48637

RECIPE

TREACLE BOLLY

This steamed pudding is another recipe with connections to Marlborough. It is named after a footpath called Treacle Bolly that runs parallel to the River Kennet near Marlborough College, the public school in the town. The spot gets very muddy after rain and is popularly said to have got its name in the mid 19th century from a miller at the nearby Kings Mill (seen in the background of this photograph, but now gone) who used to drive his cart along there, urging his fat, mottled pony on through the sticky mud with the entreaty 'Git up, old treacle bolly (belly)'. The boys from Marlborough College likened the stodgy steamed puddings served in the College dining room to the thick, heavy consistency of the mud of the spot, and gave them the nickname of 'bolly'.

MARLBOROUGH, TREACLE BOLLY 1907 57849

This pudding would originally have been made with black treacle but golden syrup is used here instead, which gives a lighter, sweeter pudding with a more delicate flavour that will probably be more to modern tastes.

175g/6oz self-raising flour
75g/3oz shredded suet
50g/2oz caster sugar
1 egg
About 150ml/5fl oz/¼ pint milk
3 rounded tablespoonfuls golden syrup

Grease a 1.2 litre (2 pint) pudding basin. Mix together the flour, suet and sugar. Make a well in the centre and add the egg and enough milk to give a soft dropping consistency. Spoon the treacle or syrup into the bottom of the prepared pudding basin, then spoon in the pudding mixture. Cover the basin with a lid made of pleated kitchen foil (to allow room for expansion during cooking), buttered on the pudding side, then a further piece of pleated foil, and tie down firmly with string. Place the basin in the top half of steamer over boiling water, or stand it in a large saucepan filled with boiling water to a third of the way up its side, bring the water back to the boil, cover the pan with its lid and steam the pudding for 1½-2 hours, adding more boiling water when necessary, to stop it boiling dry. Lift the basin from the pan, remove the lids and carefully invert the pudding onto a deep serving dish, large enough to catch the syrupy sauce as the pudding is turned out. Serve with custard or cream.

RECIPE

Malmesbury Pudding

This recipe from Malmesbury is for a good old-fashioned steamed pudding, stuffed with dried fruit and filled with a sweet, syrupy sauce. When turning this out from the basin, make sure you use a serving dish deep enough to catch the sauce that spills out when the pudding is cut open.

> 175g/6oz self-raising flour
> A pinch of salt
> 75g/3oz shredded suet
> 75g/3oz sultanas and/or raisins
> Grated zest of a lemon
> 1 dessertspoonful lemon juice
> 115g/4oz butter
> 225g/8oz soft brown sugar

Butter a pudding basin of 900ml (1½ pints) capacity. Sift the flour and salt into a mixing bowl, then add the suet, the dried fruit and the lemon zest. Add just enough cold water to mix it all to a fairly stiff dough. Cut off one-third of the dough and put it aside. Roll out the remaining dough on a lightly floured surface and use it to line the pudding basin – this is easiest to do if you roll out a large round circle of dough and then cut out a wedge before fitting the dough into the basin, pressing the cut edges of the dough together firmly to seal them. Cut the butter into small pieces and put them in the lined pudding basin, then cover with the sugar and sprinkle over the lemon juice. Roll out the remaining dough to make a lid, dampen the edge and fit it over the pudding, sealing the edges of dough together very well. Cover the basin with a lid made of a piece of buttered kitchen foil, pleated to allow room for expansion during cooking, then a further piece of pleated foil, and tie down firmly with string. Place the basin in the top half of a steamer over a saucepan of boiling water, or stand it in a saucepan filled with boiling water to halfway up its side, bring the water back to the boil and cover the pan with its lid, and steam the pudding for 2-2½ hours. Add more boiling water to the pan during the cooking time if necessary, to stop it boiling dry. Lift the basin from the pan, remove the foil and carefully invert the pudding onto a deep serving dish. Serve with cream or custard.

**MALMESBURY
THE MARKET CROSS
c1955** M13301

RECIPES

APPLE PUDDING

175g/6oz self-raising flour
50g/2oz shredded suet
A pinch of salt
50g/2oz sugar
1 egg, beaten
150ml/¼ pint milk
1 cooking apple, peeled, cored and chopped into small pieces

Pre-heat the oven to 180°C/350°F/Gas Mark 4. Grease an ovenproof dish about 20cms (8ins) square or equivalent. Mix together the flour, suet, salt and sugar. Stir in the beaten egg and the milk to form a fairly stiff mixture, then mix in the chopped apple. Turn the mixture into the prepared tin, and bake in the pre-heated oven for 50-60 minutes, until the pudding is firm to the touch. Serve hot or cold, with custard or cream.

CORSHAM, HUDSWELL 1907 57805

ELDERFLOWER PANCAKES

In late spring and early summer, the hedges of the Wiltshire countryside are festooned with creamy clusters of elderflowers. The beautifully-scented creamy sprays of elder blossoms give a delicious, delicate muscatel flavour to whatever they are cooked with. These rich pancakes flavoured with elderflowers make a delicious seasonal dessert. Serves 4.

> 8 heads of elderflowers (allowing 2 per person)
> 115g/4oz plain flour
> A pinch of salt
> 2 eggs, and two extra egg yolks
> 25g/1oz caster sugar
> 150ml/¼ pint single cream
> 150ml/¼ pint milk
> Unsalted butter for frying
> Extra caster sugar to finish
> Lemon wedges to serve

Put the eggs and egg yolks into a bowl, add the 25g/1oz of caster sugar and whisk together until the sugar has dissolved. Beat in the cream and the milk. Sift the flour and salt into another bowl and gradually blend the egg mixture into the flour, a little at a time and beating well after each addition, to make a batter with a thin, light dropping consistency. Shake the elderflower clusters to remove any insects that might be lurking, and make sure they are dry. Use a fork to comb the clusters and strip the flowers into the batter, and mix well. Leave the batter to 'rest' and infuse the flavour for at least 30 minutes. Heat a frying pan over a high heat, and add a small piece of butter. Drop in a tablespoonful of the batter and tilt the pan to spread it over the base. Fry the pancake until the underside is golden brown, then flip it over and cook the other side – this should take about one minute on each side. Drain on kitchen paper, and repeat until all the batter is used up, adding a little more butter to the pan between pancakes as necessary. Stack the cooked pancakes on top of each other and keep them warm until you have finished cooking. Serve the pancakes hot, sprinkled with caster sugar and lemon juice.

RECIPE

FRUMENTY

Frumenty (also known as furmenty or furmity) is a very old dish that is rather like a cross between porridge and rice pudding, and is flavoured with spices, honey and brandy. It was a very popular dish for special occasions in the past, such as Christmas and Easter, and in Wiltshire it was traditionally served on Mothering Sunday. It can be eaten either at breakfast or as a creamy dessert for a main meal. Frumenty is properly made with whole wheat grains that have been husked, hulled or 'pearled', but whole wheat grains are very hard to find in shops nowadays, even in health food stores, so this recipe uses pearl barley instead, which is readily available and gives similar results; however, if you can find whole wheat grains, use them in the same way as the pearl barley in this recipe. This amount serves 4 people.

> 115g/4oz pearl barley
> 900ml/1½ pints milk for soaking the pearl barley, plus a
>   further 150ml/5fl oz/¼ pint for the cooking process
> 2 tablespoonfuls brandy
> 50g/2oz raisins
> 50g/2oz sultanas
> ¼ teaspoonful freshly grated nutmeg
> ½ teaspoonful ground cinnamon
> 2 tablespoonfuls honey (or 50g/2oz sugar, if preferred)
> 150ml/5fl oz/¼ pint double cream
> A little extra cream and brandy to serve

You need to start preparing frumenty the night before you need it.

Heat the oven to 110°C/225°F/Gas Mark ¼. Put the 900ml/1½ pints of milk in a pan, bring it to the boil, then pour it into a large ovenproof dish. Stir in the pearl barley and cover the dish with its lid. Cook in the pre-heated oven for 1 hour, then turn off the heat and leave the dish in the warm oven overnight. When ready to use, the grains should have soaked up most of the milk and become soft and puffy.

Whilst the barley is cooking, soak the dried fruit in the brandy for several hours (or overnight).

When ready to prepare the frumenty, turn the pearl barley and any remaining milk into a large saucepan. Add another 150ml/5fl oz/¼ pint of milk, together with the honey or sugar, spices, soaked dried fruit and any remaining brandy. Mix it well together, breaking up any lumps. Gently bring it to the boil, stirring frequently so that nothing sticks to the bottom of the pan, then reduce the heat to low, stir in the cream and simmer for 30-45 minutes, stirring regularly as the mixture goes creamy and thickens to the desired consistency – the longer you can take over this, the better the frumenty will be.

When ready, serve the frumenty in individual bowls, with a little extra nutmeg or cinnamon sprinkled on top and perhaps some extra cream poured over. For those who want it, their helping of frumenty can also be laced with a little extra brandy.

Frumenty can be made in advance if necessary, then reheated gently when required. Any leftover frumenty is also very good eaten cold.

CASTLE COMBE, THE VILLAGE STREAM 1907 57832

The pretty town of Devizes is noted for its Georgian architecture and spacious market place, the largest in the west of England. John Britton wrote in his 'Beauties of Wiltshire' in 1801 that the market place in Devizes 'is supplied every Thursday with all kinds of corn, wool, cheese, cattle etc from the adjacent country'. Devizes was once one of the premier corn markets in the kingdom, a fact reflected by the statue of Ceres, the Roman goddess of agriculture, grain and harvests, which stands atop the handsome Corn Exchange in the market place, seen in the centre of this photograph, where local farmers came to sell their grain to the corn merchants. In the 18th and 19th centuries Devizes also became a busy coaching town as it lay on the main coaching route from Bath to London; it had a number of coaching inns, including the Bear Hotel, also seen in this view, which was the most popular stopping-off point for travellers.

One of the stagecoach travellers who stopped off at Devizes was the novelist Jane Austen, who stayed overnight at one of the town's coaching inns with her niece and nephew, Fanny and Edward Knight, on their way to Bath on the 16th of May 1799. She recorded her visit and the excellent meal she and the children enjoyed there in a letter she wrote to her sister Cassandra the next day: 'Our journey yesterday went off exceedingly well; nothing occurred to alarm or delay us. We found the road in excellent order, had very good horses all the way, and reached Devizes with ease by four o'clock… At Devizes we had comfortable rooms and a good dinner, to which we sat down about five; amongst other things we had asparagus and lobster…and some cheesecakes, on which the children made so delightful a supper as to endear the town of Devizes to them for a long time.'

Devizes was famous for centuries for its cheesecakes, but they were not the creamy desserts on a biscuit base that most people think of as cheesecakes nowadays. Two different versions of cheesecakes appear to have been associated with the town. A very old recipe for one large, pudding-style cheesecake baked in a pastry case probably originated from the cheesemaking tradition of the local area, using

a soft curd cheese known as 'Little Wilts Cheese' and mixing it with butter, eggs, sugar, spices and ground almonds; the other version is for the small, individual tart-style cheesecakes that were made to a secret recipe and sold by the Strong family at their bakery and café called The Original Cheesecake which used to be in the market place. The last member of the Strong family to make these cheesecakes, Mr Leonard Strong, left the recipe to local historian Mr Dave Buxton after his death in the late 1990s; Mr Buxton later released the recipe so the cheesecakes could be made for the Devizes Food and Drink Festival in 2010.

Recipes for both types of Devizes Cheesecake are given on the following pages. It isn't known for sure which version was the cheesecake that Jane Austen and her niece and nephew enjoyed so much, so you'll just have to make them both and see which one you like best!

DEVIZES, THE BEAR HOTEL 1898 42301

RECIPE

DEVIZES CHEESECAKE

This makes one large baked 'cheesecake' to eat warm as a pudding dish. Curd cheese as used in the original recipe is hard to find now, but good alternatives are soft cream cheeses such as Philadephia, Quark or Ricotta. This recipe also calls for orange flower (or blossom) water, which is sold in Waitrose supermarkets if you can't find it anywhere else – look for it with the food colourings and flavourings. Serves 6-8.

275g/10oz prepared puff or shortcrust pastry, as preferred
250g/9oz curd cheese, or alternative soft cream cheese – see above
175g/6oz butter, softened to room temperature
3 eggs, plus 2 extra egg yolks, beaten
2 tablespoonfuls orange flower (or blossom) water
115g/4oz ground almonds
A pinch of ground mace
115g/4oz caster sugar
¼ teaspoonful almond essence
150ml/5 fl oz/¼ pint single cream

Pre-heat the oven to 200°C/400°F/Gas Mark 6, grease a steep-sided flan tin or dish 23-26cms (9-10ins) in diameter, and line with the rolled out pastry. Line the pastry case with foil or baking paper, fill with baking beans or dry rice and bake blind for 15 minutes. Remove the beans and paper and bake for another 5 minutes for the base to dry out. Reduce the oven temperature to 180°C/350°F/Gas Mark 4. Cream together the curd or soft cheese and softened butter. Gradually beat in the sugar, eggs, ground almonds, orange flower water, almond essence and ground mace, then add the cream and mix well together. Pour into the pastry case and bake at the reduced temperature for 35-40 minutes, until the filling is risen and firm to the touch. Leave to settle for a few minutes before serving warm.

RECIPE

DEVIZES CHEESECAKES

This is adapted from the version of Devizes Cheesecakes that used to be made by Strong's bakery in the town. The filling in the original recipe was made with junket, which is warmed milk set with rennet to become curds and whey. However, rennet is not easy to find nowadays, so this version uses thick, natural Greek yogurt instead. This should make 18 small tart-style cheesecakes.

340g/12oz prepared puff pastry
115g/4oz caster sugar
115g/4oz leftover cake, broken into crumbs
½ teaspoonful ground nutmeg
25g/1oz butter, softened to room temperature
1 egg, beaten
1 x 200g pot natural thick Greek-style yogurt
1 tablespoonful currants

Pre-heat the oven to 190°C/375°F/Gas Mark 5. Grease 18 patty tins. Roll out the pastry very thinly. Use a cutter 9cms (3½ inches) in diameter to cut out 18 rounds and line the patty tins. Put the sugar, cake crumbs and nutmeg into a bowl, and rub in the butter. Mix in the beaten egg and then the yogurt, and finally stir in the currants. Half fill the lined patty tins with the mixture – it is important not to over-fill them. Bake in the pre-heated oven for about 25 minutes, until the filling is risen, firm to the touch and golden, but not over-browned. Leave the cheesecakes to settle in the tin for 5 minutes then turn onto a wire rack to cool, when the filling will sink down a little. Serve warm or cold.

RECIPE

APPLE CROWDIES

'Apple Crowdy' is the Wiltshire dialect name for an apple turnover. This quantity should make 6-8 Apple Crowdies at this size.

>2 large cooking apples
>3 whole cloves
>15g/½ oz butter
>Grated zest of half a lemon
>115g/4oz soft brown or caster sugar
>1 tablespoonful sultanas (optional)
>450g/1 lb prepared weight of puff pastry or
>sweet shortcrust pastry, as preferred
>A little milk or egg white, to finish
>A little extra caster sugar, to finish

Peel, core and chop the apples. Melt the butter in a saucepan and add the apples, lemon zest and cloves. Cover the pan with its lid and cook very slowly over a gentle heat, stirring occasionally, so the apples cook and soften but do not brown or burn – this will take 20 to 30 minutes. When the apples are cooked and soft, remove from the heat and take out the cloves. Beat the apples to a puree, and stir in the sugar and sultanas, if using. Set aside and leave the mixture to cool completely.

Pre-heat the oven to 200°C/400°F/Gas Mark 6 and grease a baking tray. Roll out the pastry to about 5mm (¼ inch) thick. Cut out 6-8 rounds about 15cms (6 ins) in diameter – use a saucer or suchlike to cut around. Place a tablespoonful of the mixture in the middle of each round, leaving a good margin round the edge. Dampen the edges of each round by brushing it with water, then bring up one half of each round over the filling and turn it over to the other side, to make a half-moon shape. Seal the edges well by pinching them together with a finger and thumb. Brush each Crowdie with a little milk or lightly beaten egg white and sprinkle with a little caster sugar. Place the Crowdies on the greased baking sheet and bake just above the centre of the pre-heated oven for 25-30 minutes, until golden brown. These can be eaten eat either warm or cold.

RECIPE

BUTTERMILK CAKE

Buttermilk is a by-product of butter-making and was often an ingredient of cake-making in the past, as when it is used with bicarbonate of soda it helps to lighten the dough. There are recipes for Buttermilk Cake from all over the country, but this spiced version is from Wiltshire. It results in a very nice rich fruit cake with a spongy texture and good flavour. Buttermilk is rather like runny yogurt and can be found in most large supermarkets – look for it in the cream section. If buttermilk proves hard to find, use soured milk, either bought or made at home by stirring 2 teaspoonfuls of lemon juice into 300ml (½ pint) of milk, then setting it aside for 1 hour to set.

450g/1 lb plain flour
½ teaspoonful bicarbonate of soda
½ teaspoonful each of ground ginger, mixed spice
   and ground cinnamon
225g/8oz butter or margarine
225g/8oz soft brown sugar (light or dark brown, as you prefer)
450/1 lb mixed dried fruit – currants, raisins, sultanas
2 eggs, lightly beaten
300ml/½ pint buttermilk or soured milk (see above)

Pre-heat the oven to 180°C/350°F/Gas Mark 4. Grease and line a round cake tin 20cms (8ins) in diameter. Sift the flour, bicarbonate of soda and spices into a large mixing bowl. Rub in the butter or margarine until the mixture resembles fine breadcrumbs. Stir in the sugar and dried fruit, then mix in the lightly beaten eggs and the buttermilk and combine it all well together. Turn the mixture into the prepared cake tin and smooth the surface. Bake in the centre of the pre-heated oven for one hour, then cover the top of the cake with a piece of kitchen foil to prevent it browning too much, reduce the oven temperature to 160°C/325°F/Gas Mark 3, and bake for a further 45-50 minutes. Take the cake out of the oven and leave in the tin to settle for at least 15 minutes before turning it out onto a wire tray to cool completely. Like most fruit cakes, this is best kept until the next day before eating.

RECIPE

LARDY CAKE

This cake is famously associated with Wiltshire, and originates from the county's pig-keeping tradition – its key ingredient is lard, the fat that was rendered down when a pig was killed and stored for future use. Lard was the most widely available cooking fat to housewives and bakers in the past and was often used in baking instead of butter, which is much more expensive. Lardy Cake is made from yeasted bread dough that is rolled and folded several times over layers of lard, sugar and dried fruit, and was often made on baking day, using up any leftover bread dough to make a tasty treat for teatime. When baked, Lardy Cake has a delicious crispy, sticky crust. This recipe comes from Chippenham, and enriches the dough with an added egg.

225g/8oz strong white breadmaking flour
1 x 7g sachet (½ oz, or 1½ teaspoonfuls) easy-bake
   fast-action dried yeast
150ml/¼ pint milk
1 teaspoonful sugar
1 egg, beaten
115g/4oz lard or white cooking fat, cut into very small pieces,
   softened (or half lard and half butter can be used if preferred)
115g/4oz granulated or caster sugar
115g/4oz currants, or a mixture of currants and sultanas

Sift the flour into a mixing bowl, and stir in the dried yeast. Put the milk in a saucepan and warm gently to blood heat. Add the teaspoonful of sugar and stir until dissolved. Add the milk to the beaten egg and mix well, then pour the mixture into the flour and mix it together well to form a soft dough. Turn the dough onto a lightly floured surface and knead for 10 minutes or so, until it is smooth and elastic. Return the dough to the bowl, cover with a damp tea towel or put the bowl inside

a polythene bag, and leave in a warm place for about one hour for the dough to rise and double in size.

Knock back the risen dough, then roll it out quite thinly on a floured surface to an oblong shape, about 30cms (12ins) by 15cms (6ins). Dot one third of the lard over two thirds of the dough (or spread it, if it is soft enough), then sprinkle over one third of the sugar and then one third of the dried fruit. Fold the un-spread third of the dough over half the filled portion of dough, and then fold the remaining third on top of that, making a three-layered 'dough sandwich'. Seal the open ends of the dough parcel by pressing down on them with the rolling pin. Give the piece of dough a half turn and gently roll it out into a thin oblong shape again, and repeat the whole procedure once more with another third of lard, sugar and dried fruit, then repeat it all once more for a final process of spreading and layering.

Grease a baking tin about 20cms (8ins) square, or a rectangular tin about 25 x 15cms (10 x 6ins). Gently roll out the filled parcel of dough to make a shape the same size and place it in the baking tin, pressing the edges to fit it neatly. Cover the tin with a damp tea towel, or place in the polythene bag, and leave for a further 30 minutes for the dough to rise again.

Pre-heat the oven to 200°C/400°F/Gas Mark 6. When the dough has risen, bake the cake in the pre-heated oven for 30-40 minutes, until it is crispy and golden brown.

Leave the cake to stand in the tin for 10 minutes, then use two forks to lift it out of the tin, flip it over and place it on a plate the other way up, so the side that was at the bottom of the tin and has the sticky sugary coating is on top. Leave to cool down for a few minutes before cutting into squares and serving – lardy cake is at its best eaten whilst it is still warm from the oven.

RECIPE

EASTER CAKES

These thick fruited biscuits are called cakes in Wiltshire, and were traditionally baked at Easter time. They are made with a butter-rich short dough lightly flavoured with spices. This amount should make about 18 Easter Cakes at this size.

> 115g/4oz butter
> 75g/3oz caster sugar
> 2 eggs, separated
> 225g/8oz self-raising flour
> ½ teaspoonful ground mixed spice
> ½ teaspoonful ground cinnamon
> 50g/2oz currants
> 1-2 tablespoonfuls milk
> Extra caster sugar to finish

Pre-heat the oven to 180°C/350°F/Gas Mark 4. Grease 2 baking sheets, or line with baking paper.

Beat together the butter and sugar until light and fluffy, then beat in the 2 egg yolks. Sift the flour and spices over the mixture, add the currants and use a round-bladed knife to mix it all together, adding just enough milk to form quite a firm dough. Gather the dough into a ball in your hand, then gently roll it out on a lightly floured surface to about 1cm (½ inch) thick. Cut it into rounds with a fluted biscuit cutter 6.5cms (2½ ins) in diameter. Arrange the rounds slightly apart on the baking sheets. Lightly whisk the egg whites with a fork. Liberally brush the top of each round with the beaten egg white and sprinkle with a little extra caster sugar, to make a crispy topping. Bake in the pre-heated oven for 15-20 minutes, until crisp and golden, but not over-browned. Remove from the oven and leave the rounds on the baking sheets for five minutes to settle and firm up, then transfer to a wire rack to cool completely.

RECIPE

FAIRINGS

Crisp, spicy biscuits such as these were treats sold at town and country fairs in the past, where livestock was sold and workers were hired for the coming year. This amount makes about 30 biscuits, which develop a pretty crinkled surface as they bake. Be very careful about measuring the syrup, as if you overdo it the dough will be too moist and the biscuits will spread and flatten too much during the cooking time, becoming a sheet of sticky dough rather than individual round biscuits!

3 level tablespoonfuls golden syrup
225g/8oz plain flour
1 teaspoonful bicarbonate of soda
1 teaspoonful ground ginger
1 teaspoonful mixed spice
115g/4oz butter or margarine, diced
115g/4oz caster sugar

Pre-heat the oven to 180°C/350°F/Gas Mark 4. Grease 2 baking sheets, or line with baking paper. Warm the syrup in a pan over a gentle heat until it is runny. Remove from the heat and leave it to cool a little. Sift the flour, bicarbonate of soda, ground ginger and mixed spice into a mixing bowl. Rub in the butter or margarine until the mixture resembles fine breadcrumbs, then stir in the sugar. Add the cooled syrup into the flour mixture and mix it together well to form a stiff dough. Flour your hands and roll small pieces of the dough between your palms, to form small balls about the size of a walnut. Place the balls on the baking sheets, well spaced out to allow them room to spread whilst cooking without touching each other. (You may need to cook the biscuits in several batches.) Bake in the centre of the pre-heated oven for 10-12 minutes, until they are risen and golden brown – be careful not to overcook them and let them get too browned, or they will be rock-hard when they cool. Leave the biscuits on the baking sheets to cool and firm up for a few minutes, then carefully transfer them to a wire rack to cool completely, when they will become crisp. Store in an airtight container.

RECIPE

WILTSHIRE BACON SCONES

These savoury scones can be either served on their own, perhaps at breakfast or teatime, as an accompaniment to soup, and in picnics or a packed lunch. They are delicious warm from the oven, perhaps split in half and spread with butter, but are also good eaten cold – try them split in half and spread with a herby cream cheese. This is based on a traditional recipe from Wiltshire for a savoury teabread which is made in a 900g/2 lb loaf tin and baked for about one hour, but the mixture is used here to make individual rustic-style scones which are quicker to bake. This amount should make 12 scones.

115g/4oz bacon rashers
450g/1 lb self-raising flour
1 level teaspoonful mustard powder
50g/2oz margarine (or, more authentically, lard or dripping)
4 sticks of celery, trimmed, peeled and finely chopped
1 onion, peeled and very finely chopped
Salt and freshly ground black pepper
2 tablespoonfuls finely chopped fresh parsley
1 egg, beaten
About 300ml/½ pint milk

Pre-heat the oven to 200°C/400°F/Gas Mark 6 and grease two baking sheets.

De-rind the bacon, chop it into small pieces and dry-fry it in its own fat in a fairly large frying pan for a few minutes. Add the finely chopped celery and onion and cook for about 5 minutes, until the vegetables are softened. Put the pan to one side and leave the mixture to cool.

BISHOPSTONE, POST OFFICE AND STORES 1908 B298001

Sift the flour and mustard powder into a bowl, and season well with salt and freshly ground black pepper. Rub in the margarine (or lard or dripping) until the mixture resembles fine breadcrumbs. Add the chopped parsley, and then stir in the bacon mixture.

Beat the egg, and add enough milk to make it up to 300ml/½ pint, then stir this into the mixture. Mix it all together with a round-bladed knife to form a dough. Gather the dough into a ball and knead it gently on a lightly floured surface, then form the dough into 12 roughly-shaped rounds. Place them on the baking trays, spaced well apart, lightly dust with flour, and bake in the pre-heated oven for 20-25 minutes, until they are risen and golden brown and sound hollow when tapped on the bottom. Leave the scones to rest on the baking sheets for two minutes before transferring them to a wire rack.

FRANCIS FRITH

PIONEER VICTORIAN PHOTOGRAPHER

Francis Frith, founder of the world-famous photographic archive, was a complex and multi-talented man. A devout Quaker and a highly successful Victorian businessman, he was philosophical by nature and pioneering in outlook. By 1855 he had already established a wholesale grocery business in Liverpool, and sold it for the astonishing sum of £200,000, which is the equivalent today of over £15,000,000. Now in his thirties, and captivated by the new science of photography, Frith set out on a series of pioneering journeys up the Nile and to the Near East.

INTRIGUE AND EXPLORATION

He was the first photographer to venture beyond the sixth cataract of the Nile. Africa was still the mysterious 'Dark Continent', and Stanley and Livingstone's historic meeting was a decade into the future. The conditions for picture taking confound belief. He laboured for hours in his wicker dark-room in the sweltering heat of the desert, while the volatile chemicals fizzed dangerously in their trays. Back in London he exhibited his photographs and was 'rapturously cheered' by members of the Royal Society. His reputation as a photographer was made overnight.

VENTURE OF A LIFE-TIME

By the 1870s the railways had threaded their way across the country, and Bank Holidays and half-day Saturdays had been made obligatory by Act of Parliament. All of a sudden the working man and his family were able to enjoy days out, take holidays, and see a little more of the world.

With typical business acumen, Francis Frith foresaw that these new tourists would enjoy having souvenirs to commemorate their days out. For the next thirty years he travelled the country by train and by pony and trap, producing fine photographs of seaside resorts and beauty spots that were keenly bought by millions of Victorians. These prints were painstakingly pasted into family albums and pored over during the dark nights of winter, rekindling precious memories of summer excursions. Frith's studio was soon supplying retail shops all over the country, and by 1890 F Frith & Co had become the greatest specialist photographic publishing company in the world, with over 2,000 sales outlets, and pioneered the picture postcard.

FRANCIS FRITH'S LEGACY

Francis Frith had died in 1898 at his villa in Cannes, his great project still growing. By 1970 the archive he created contained over a third of a million pictures showing 7,000 British towns and villages.

Frith's legacy to us today is of immense significance and value, for the magnificent archive of evocative photographs he created provides a unique record of change in the cities, towns and villages throughout Britain over a century and more. Frith and his fellow studio photographers revisited locations many times down the years to update their views, compiling for us an enthralling and colourful pageant of British life and character.

We are fortunate that Frith was dedicated to recording the minutiae of everyday life. For it is this sheer wealth of visual data, the painstaking chronicle of changes in dress, transport, street layouts, buildings, housing and landscape that captivates us so much today, offering us a powerful link with the past and with the lives of our ancestors.

Computers have now made it possible for Frith's many thousands of images to be accessed almost instantly. The archive offers every one of us an opportunity to examine the places where we and our families have lived and worked down the years. Its images, depicting our shared past, are now bringing pleasure and enlightenment to millions around the world a century and more after his death.

For further information visit: www.francisfrith.com

INTERIOR DECORATION

Frith's photographs can be seen framed and as giant wall murals in thousands of pubs, restaurants, hotels, banks, retail stores and other public buildings throughout Britain. These provide interesting and attractive décor, generating strong local interest and acting as a powerful reminder of gentler days in our increasingly busy and frenetic world.

FRITH PRODUCTS

All Frith photographs are available as prints and posters in a variety of different sizes and styles. In the UK we also offer a range of other gift and stationery products illustrated with Frith photographs, although many of these are not available for delivery outside the UK – see our web site for more information on the products available for delivery in your country.

THE INTERNET

Over 100,000 photographs of Britain can be viewed and purchased on the Frith web site. The web site also includes memories and reminiscences contributed by our customers, who have personal knowledge of localities and of the people and properties depicted in Frith photographs. If you wish to learn more about a specific town or village you may find these reminiscences fascinating to browse. Why not add your own comments if you think they would be of interest to others? See **www.francisfrith.com**

PLEASE HELP US BRING FRITH'S PHOTOGRAPHS TO LIFE

Our authors do their best to recount the history of the places they write about. They give insights into how particular towns and villages developed, they describe the architecture of streets and buildings, and they discuss the lives of famous people who lived there. But however knowledgeable our authors are, the story they tell is necessarily incomplete.

Frith's photographs are so much more than plain historical documents. They are living proofs of the flow of human life down the generations. They show real people at real moments in history; and each of those people is the son or daughter of someone, the brother or sister, aunt or uncle, grandfather or grandmother of someone else. All of them lived, worked and played in the streets depicted in Frith's photographs.

We would be grateful if you would give us your insights into the places shown in our photographs: the streets and buildings, the shops, businesses and industries. Post your memories of life in those streets on the Frith website: what it was like growing up there, who ran the local shop and what shopping was like years ago; if your workplace is shown tell us about your working day and what the building is used for now. Read other visitors' memories and reconnect with your shared local history and heritage. With your help more and more Frith photographs can be brought to life, and vital memories preserved for posterity, and for the benefit of historians in the future.

Wherever possible, we will try to include some of your comments in future editions of our books. Moreover, if you spot errors in dates, titles or other facts, please let us know, because our archive records are not always completely accurate—they rely on 140 years of human endeavour and hand-compiled records. You can email us using the contact form on the website.

Thank you!

For further information, trade, or author enquiries
please contact us at the address below:

**The Francis Frith Collection, Oakley Business Park,
Wylye Road, Dinton, Wiltshire SP3 5EU England.**
Tel: +44 (0)1722 716 376 Fax: +44 (0)1722 716 881
e-mail: sales@francisfrith.co.uk **www.francisfrith.com**